D0021856

MINECRAFT™

NEW YORK

Stay safe online. Any website addresses listed in this book are correct at the time of going to print. However, Del Rey is not responsible for content hosted by third parties. Please be aware that online content can be subject to change and websites can contain content that is unsuitable for children. We advise that all children are supervised when using the Internet. This publisher does not have any control over and does not assume any responsibility for author or third-party websites or their content.

ONLINE SAFETY FOR YOUNGER FANS
Spending time online is great fun! Here are a few simple rules to help younger fans stay safe and keep the Internet a great place to spend time:
- Never give out your real name—don't use it as your username.
- Never give out any of your personal details.
- Never tell anybody which school you go to or how old you are.
- Never tell anybody your password except a parent or a guardian.
- Be aware that you must be 13 or over to create an account on many sites. Always check the site policy and ask a parent or guardian for permission before registering.
- Always tell a parent or guardian if something is worrying you.

Copyright © 2022 by Mojang AB. All Rights Reserved. Minecraft, the MINECRAFT logo and the MOJANG STUDIOS logo are trademarks of the Microsoft group of companies.

Published in the United States by Del Rey, an imprint of Random House, a division of Penguin Random House LLC, New York.

DEL REY and the CIRCLE colophon are registered trademarks of Penguin Random House LLC.

Originally published in hardcover in the United Kingdom by Farshore, an imprint of HarperCollins Publishers Limited.

ISBN 978-0-593-49760-9
Ebook ISBN 978-0-593-49761-6

Printed in China on acid-free paper by C & C Offset

randomhousebooks.com

4 6 8 9 7 5

First US Edition

Special thanks to Sherin Kwan, Alex Wiltshire and Milo Bengtsson.

MINECRAFT™

AMAZING
BITE-SIZE
BUILDS

OVER 20 AWESOME MINI-PROJECTS

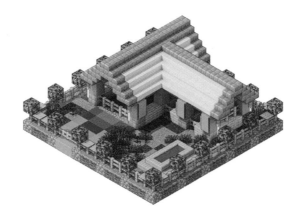

CONTENTS

INTRODUCTION

Welcome to *Amazing Bite-Size Builds*! This book is packed with fun mini-projects for you to build in Minecraft. From marine tugboats to hanging homes and even a parkour course, there's a build for everyone between these pages!

Whether you're a beginner or an experienced player, there's always more to learn when you're playing Minecraft! With exploded diagrams and detailed step-by-step instructions, this book will take you all the way from start to finish, helping you to complete these amazing builds with ease. The builds vary from small to large and from simple to difficult. Check out the key on each build to find out more.

This book embraces creativity, and we encourage you to put your own stamp on these builds. If you think your build will look better with different blocks or tweaked designs, follow your instincts and make these builds your own. Soon, you'll be showing off your incredible talent to the world around you.

GENERAL BUILD TIPS

The builds in this book are suitable for both beginners and experts. Whether you're a first-time player or a seasoned Minecrafter, everyone can use a few general build tips to help ensure you have a great time following the guides and completing the builds.

CREATIVE MODE

Complete these builds in Creative mode. With unlimited access to all the blocks in the game and instant block removal, Creative mode is the easiest way to build in Minecraft. If you like a challenge, each structure can be built in Survival mode – but be warned! It will take a lot more time and preparation.

BUILD PREPARATION

Before starting a build, take a moment to look at the instructions. Consider where you want to place the build and how much space you will need to complete it. Give yourself plenty of space to work.

TEMPORARY BLOCKS

Temporary building blocks are helpful for counting out spaces and placing floating items. Using temporary blocks will also help you with tricky block placement.

Count the dimensions using different color blocks. This row represents 13 blocks: 5 green + 5 yellow + 3 green.

Use temporary blocks to help place floating blocks.

HOTBARS

Most builds use lots of different blocks. You can prepare your blocks in the hotbar before starting for quick access, and if you don't have enough space, you can save up to nine hotbars in the inventory window.

Saved Hotbars

BLOCK PLACEMENT

Placing a block beside an interactive one, such as an enchanting table, can be tricky. By clicking to place a block, you'll interact with the interactive one instead. In order to place a block without interacting, first crouch and then click to place it.

UNICORN STATUE

Recreating your favorite legendary animals is lots of fun! Start with this magical unicorn, a mythical creature said to have magical powers and bring good fortune. Build this easy-to-spot statue near your stables to show everyone where to bring their rides.

DIFFICULTY:
★☆☆☆☆
🕐 10 minutes

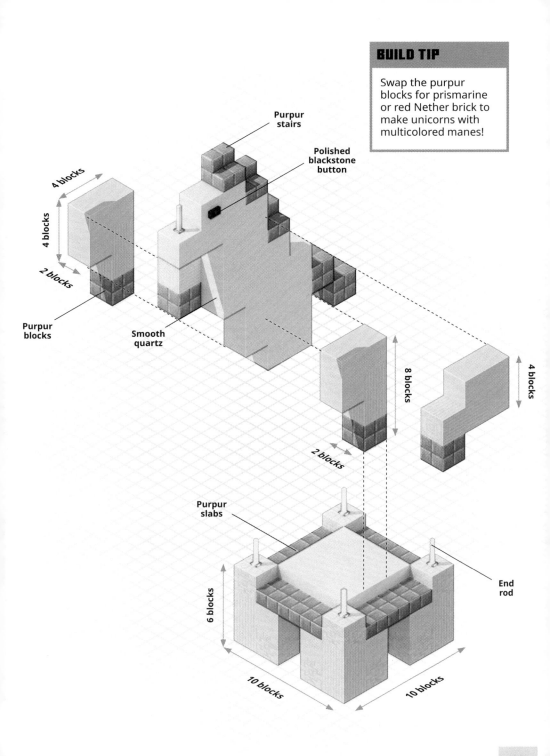

Purpur stairs

Polished blackstone button

BUILD TIP

Swap the purpur blocks for prismarine or red Nether brick to make unicorns with multicolored manes!

4 blocks

4 blocks

2 blocks

Purpur blocks

Smooth quartz

8 blocks

2 blocks

4 blocks

Purpur slabs

6 blocks

End rod

10 blocks

10 blocks

9

HILLSIDE HOME

When you find yourself in a bumpy, foresty biome, finding space to build your home can be challenging. Why not build directly into a hill? Simply dig out a space and start building! This hillside home fits snugly into any mound, making it perfect for hard-to-clear biomes.

DIFFICULTY:
★★☆☆☆
🕐 30 minutes

Start by finding a nearby hillside and excavating a 4-block-tall cave. Then lay the foundations as shown, using cobblestone, dark oak planks, stone bricks, a campfire and gray and white concrete.

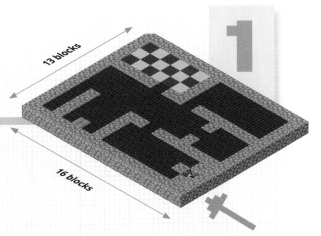

13 blocks

16 blocks

Place the campfire in the empty hearth space.

Next, use the cobblestone outline to start building the walls. Use stone, stone bricks, spruce planks, dirt and green concrete.

Continue building the walls up. Leave gaps for the doorways and windows, and fill them with glass panes and a dark oak door.

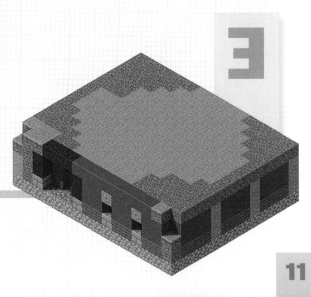

4

Next, create circular passages in the entrance and each of the corridors using spruce stairs and trapdoors, then light up the interiors to prevent mobs from spawning using lanterns. See the example shown.

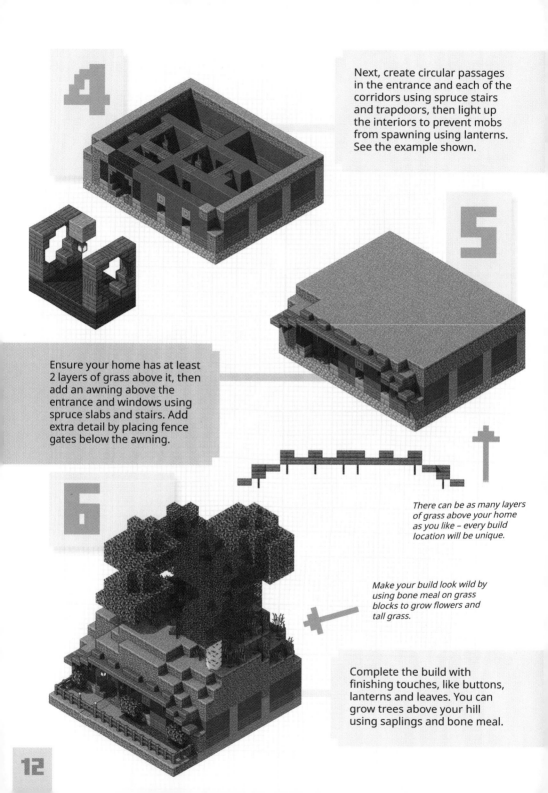

5

Ensure your home has at least 2 layers of grass above it, then add an awning above the entrance and windows using spruce slabs and stairs. Add extra detail by placing fence gates below the awning.

There can be as many layers of grass above your home as you like – every build location will be unique.

6

Make your build look wild by using bone meal on grass blocks to grow flowers and tall grass.

Complete the build with finishing touches, like buttons, lanterns and leaves. You can grow trees above your hill using saplings and bone meal.

INTERIORS

Now it's time to decorate the interiors! This build is designed to be homey, with a kitchen, bedroom and living room space. There are lots of small corners, so don't forget to light up the space to stop mobs from spawning!

Use the floor plan to see how everything fits together.

This kitchenette has a furnace and a smoker to cook all your favorite foods. Use trapdoors to create shelving units and a cauldron for a supply of water.

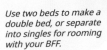

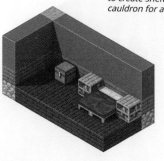

Use two beds to make a double bed, or separate into singles for rooming with your BFF.

Use barrels and chests to give yourself plenty of storage. Barrels can be stacked for most efficient storage.

A lliving room with a hearth is the perfect place to unwind after a long day. Place a book on the lectern to record your adventures.

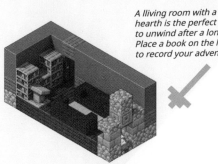

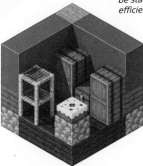

MARINE TUGBOAT

Ahoy, seafaring sailors! Are you set up for your underwater escapades? Whether you're cruising along the coast or fishing for valuables, it's important to have a boat nearby to take a break and store your newly found treasure. A tugboat may be just what you need!

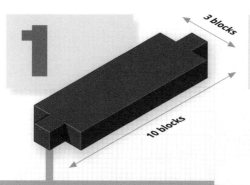

1

Start by using gray concrete to create the base of the tugboat. Build the base 2 blocks underwater so the completed tugboat sits at water level.

3 blocks

10 blocks

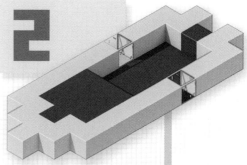

2

Build a layer directly above the base layer using gray concrete, white concrete and glass blocks.

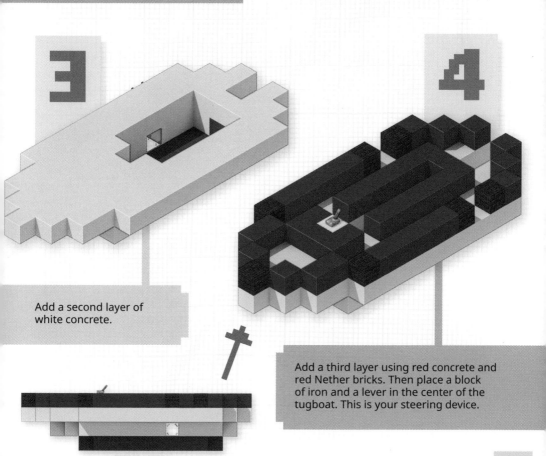

3

Add a second layer of white concrete.

SIDE VIEW

4

Add a third layer using red concrete and red Nether bricks. Then place a block of iron and a lever in the center of the tugboat. This is your steering device.

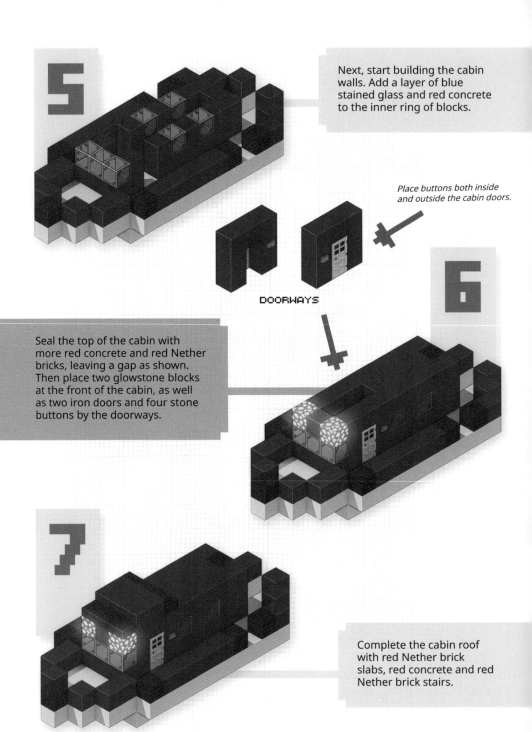

5

Next, start building the cabin walls. Add a layer of blue stained glass and red concrete to the inner ring of blocks.

Place buttons both inside and outside the cabin doors.

DOORWAYS

6

Seal the top of the cabin with more red concrete and red Nether bricks, leaving a gap as shown. Then place two glowstone blocks at the front of the cabin, as well as two iron doors and four stone buttons by the doorways.

7

Complete the cabin roof with red Nether brick slabs, red concrete and red Nether brick stairs.

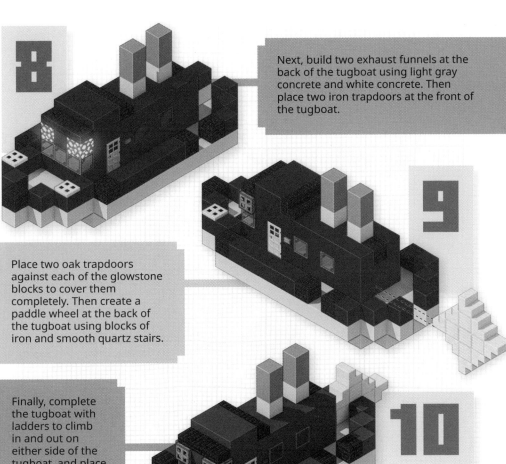

8

Next, build two exhaust funnels at the back of the tugboat using light gray concrete and white concrete. Then place two iron trapdoors at the front of the tugboat.

9

Place two oak trapdoors against each of the glowstone blocks to cover them completely. Then create a paddle wheel at the back of the tugboat using blocks of iron and smooth quartz stairs.

10

Finally, complete the tugboat with ladders to climb in and out on either side of the tugboat, and place three red Nether brick stairs in front of the cabin.

INTERIORS

Fill your tugboat with some exploration essentials. Place a bed to sleep through the night, chests for storing your enchanted underwater equipment and furnaces to keep you fully supplied with cooked food.

Advanced players may want to include a brewing table for crafting potions of Water Breathing and Night Vision.

SIDEWALK CAFE

Want a cup of milk after a long day mining? Invite your friends around for a sit-down and a chit-chat in your very own sidewalk cafe, with item frames to showcase your cooking skills. Be modern-day hipsters by drinking from flower pots while eating cake. Best of all...PETS ARE WELCOME!

DIFFICULTY:
★★★☆☆
🕑 30 minutes

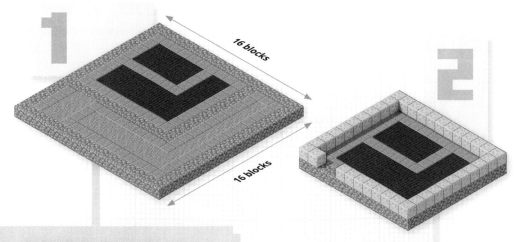

1

16 blocks

16 blocks

Start by laying the foundations for the sidewalk cafe using cobblestone, polished andesite, andesite and dark oak planks.

2

Next, start building the walls for the cafe. Place a ring of polished diorite blocks around the inner cobblestone outline.

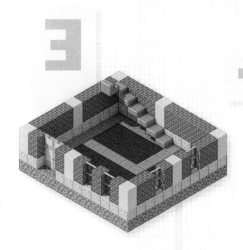

3

Extend the walls another 2 blocks taller using bricks, quartz bricks and glass panes. Then place birch doors and birch trapdoors in the entrance. Build a staircase using polished andesite slabs and stairs.

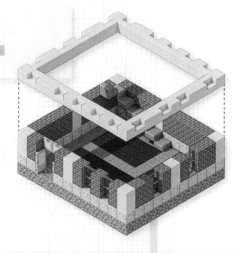

4

Add a layer of chiseled quartz and quartz stairs to the walls.

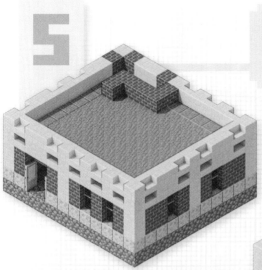

5

Create a floor for the roof terrace using andesite and polished andesite slabs. Then add another layer of bricks, quartz bricks and quartz stairs to the walls.

6

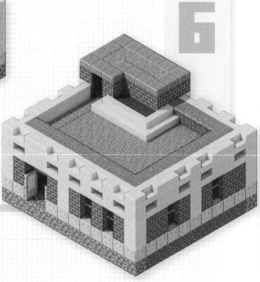

Build a brick, andesite slab and polished andesite slab roof for the staircase entrance and place a dark oak door in the doorway. Add grass blocks around the inner walls and use quartz stairs and water to create a pond.

7

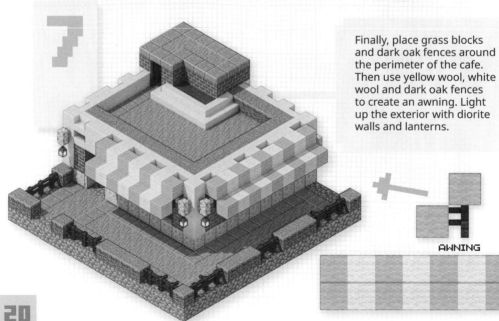

Finally, place grass blocks and dark oak fences around the perimeter of the cafe. Then use yellow wool, white wool and dark oak fences to create an awning. Light up the exterior with diorite walls and lanterns.

AWNING

CAFE DECORATIONS

Your cafe is almost ready to welcome its first customers! Before opening your doors, set up a serving counter and some tables for your patrons.

Make the cafe feel lively with some pretty flowers! Make a lectern and book for recording reservations.

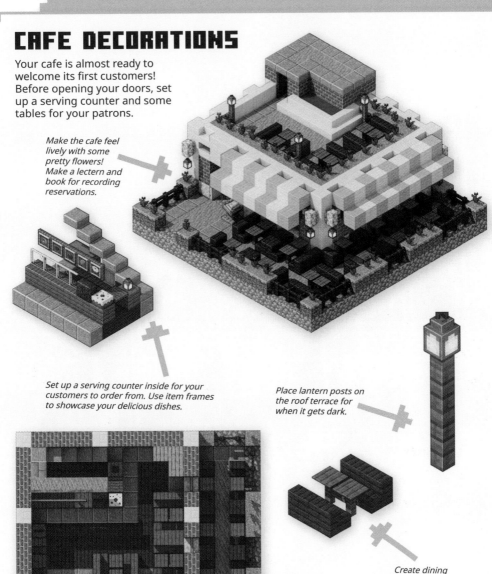

Set up a serving counter inside for your customers to order from. Use item frames to showcase your delicious dishes.

Place lantern posts on the roof terrace for when it gets dark.

Create dining tables using stairs, fences and pressure plates.

Follow the floor plan to see how the tables fit in. Need larger tables? Join two or more together!

BEE HAVEN

Did you know that bees are a vital part of our ecosystem? As pollinators, bees fly from plant to plant spreading pollen and ensuring that the planet's diversity of plant life can thrive, and in turn, so do the animals that rely on them. Build this bee habitat near your crops to help boost your yield.

DIFFICULTY:
★★☆☆☆
🕐 15 minutes

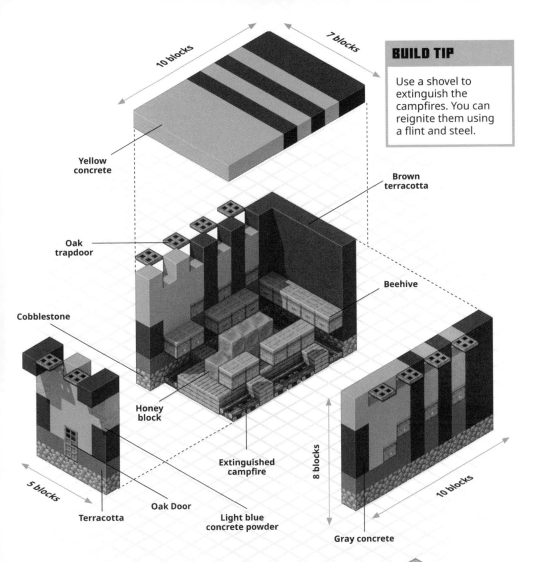

10 blocks

7 blocks

BUILD TIP

Use a shovel to extinguish the campfires. You can reignite them using a flint and steel.

Yellow concrete

Brown terracotta

Oak trapdoor

Beehive

Cobblestone

Honey block

Extinguished campfire

8 blocks

10 blocks

5 blocks

Oak Door

Terracotta

Light blue concrete powder

Gray concrete

CAMPFIRES & BEES

Bees are neutral mobs, meaning they will keep to themselves unless you attack them or touch their nests. This can make getting that sweet, sweet honey a bit tricky! Luckily, bees are calmed by smoke. When you're ready to collect the honey, light the campfires beneath your beehives to calm the bees. You will need shears to collect the honey.

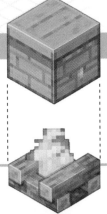

FISHING SHACK

Fishing in Minecraft works just like it does in the real world, with a chance of reeling in tasty fish, sunken treasure or, if you're unlucky, the occasional piece of junk – someone should really clean up these waters! The fishing shack will also keep you safe from drowned mobs.

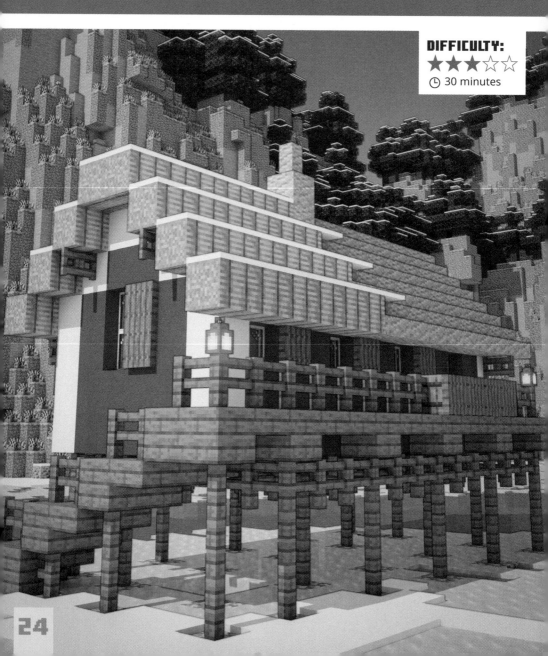

DIFFICULTY:
★★★☆☆
🕐 30 minutes

1

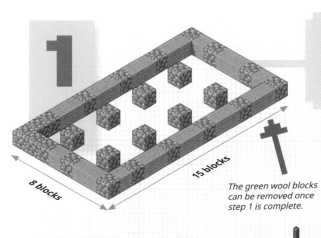

Start by laying the foundations for your fishing shack. Place the cobblestone blocks 1 block below water level and extend them down, all the way to the seabed.

8 blocks

15 blocks

The green wool blocks can be removed once step 1 is complete.

2

Build 3-block-tall spruce fence posts on each of the cobblestone blocks in the back 5 rows.

3

Join the posts together with spruce fences to create a grid.

4

This will be your fishing hole!

Next, build a floor on top of the spruce fences using spruce planks, spruce slabs, red concrete and white concrete. Leave a 2 x 2-block gap in the floor for fishing.

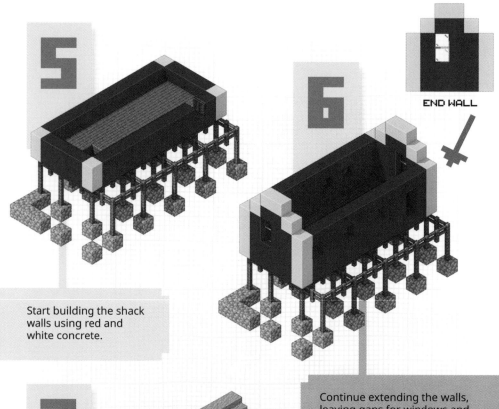

END WALL

Start building the shack walls using red and white concrete.

Continue extending the walls, leaving gaps for windows and a door as shown. Place single and double glass panes in the windows and a dark oak door in the doorway.

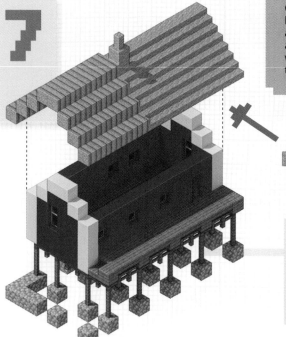

ROOF STRUCTURE

Use hay bales and andesite stairs to create a roof for the shack and make a chimney out of andesite blocks. Add spruce blocks and slabs beside the wall to create a balcony outside.

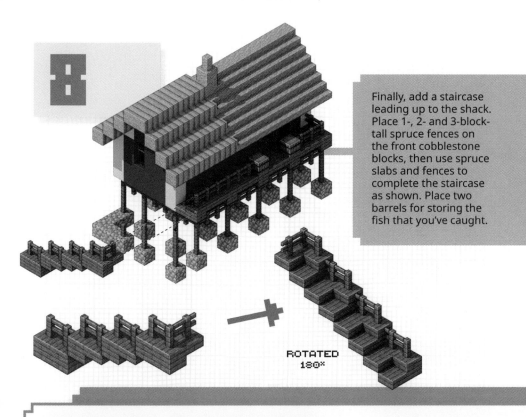

8

Finally, add a staircase leading up to the shack. Place 1-, 2- and 3-block-tall spruce fences on the front cobblestone blocks, then use spruce slabs and fences to complete the staircase as shown. Place two barrels for storing the fish that you've caught.

ROTATED
180°

INTERIOR DECORATIONS

Now to fill your fishing shack with all the fishing essentials. This layout has everything you need for a nice long fishing holiday with your friends.

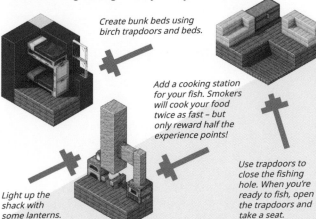

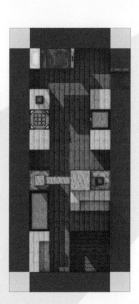

Create bunk beds using birch trapdoors and beds.

Add a cooking station for your fish. Smokers will cook your food twice as fast – but only reward half the experience points!

Light up the shack with some lanterns.

Use trapdoors to close the fishing hole. When you're ready to fish, open the trapdoors and take a seat.

EDROCK TRAI

Mining is one of the great pleasures of Minecraft. Digging caves, collecting resources, searching for diamonds – all part of the blocky fun. But getting in and out of your mine can be long and grueling. This railway will take care of the journey – see page 35 for how it works.

DIFFICULTY:
★★★★★
🕐 45 minutes

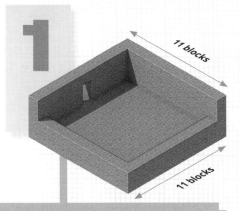

1

11 blocks

11 blocks

Start by digging a 3-block-deep chamber into the surface directly above your mine, leaving the stone walls untouched and a gap for the entrance. The walls can be composed of any blocks you find – this build uses stone.

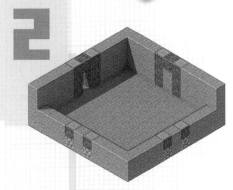

2

Replace blocks in all four walls with oak logs and cobblestone as shown. This will give your build a mine shaft feel. Create a 2-block-tall gap in one wall for the entrance.

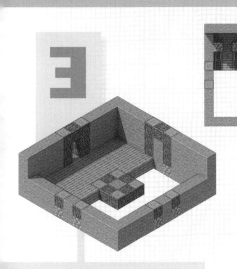

3

Remove half of the floor and create a platform for the embarking station using oak logs and oak planks.

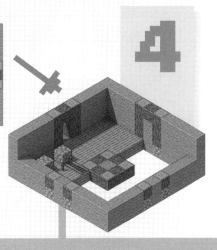

4

Next, begin the first stages of your train track. Start by placing two cobblestone blocks, two powered rails, two rails and a redstone torch to the left of the entrance as shown.

5

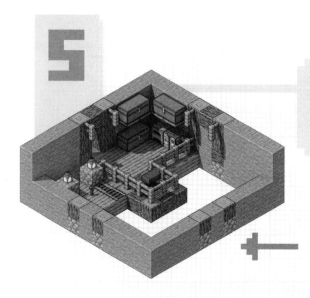

Complete the platform with some decorative details. Place an oak fence barrier, add storage chests on oak trapdoors and light up the room with lanterns.

A fence barrier will stop you from falling – it's a long way to the bottom!

SECTION 2: MINE SHAFT
DESCENDING INTO THE MINE

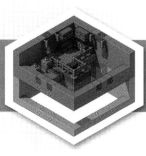

6

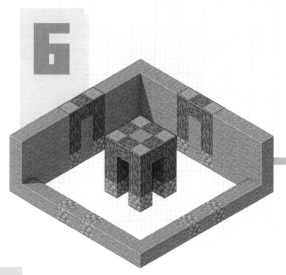

Next, it's time to build the mine shaft. Start by excavating another 4 layers of blocks directly below your embarking station, then build the cobblestone and oak log structure.

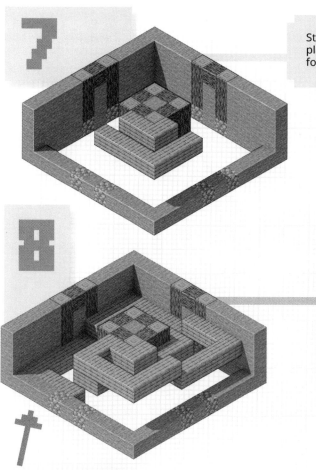

7

Start building two rings of oak planks around the central column for your railway.

8

Continue building the oak plank rings, cascading them around the inner wall and the central column to form a corkscrew shape as you descend down the mine shaft. As you go down each layer, connect the two rings with oak planks as shown in the supporting image.

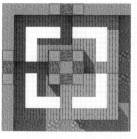

9

Now start laying the tracks with two powered rails, then add regular rails. Activate the powered rails with a redstone torch.

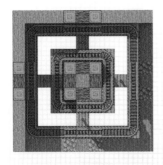

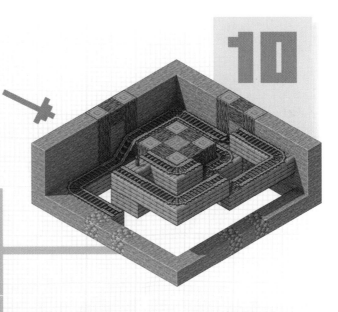

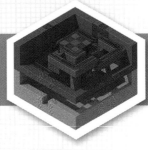

10

Continue placing powered rails and regular rails around the oak planks.

To continue deeper underground, repeat steps 6-10. Each repetition of the mine shaft section will go another four layers deeper underground.

SECTION 3: DISEMBARKING STATION END OF THE LINE

11

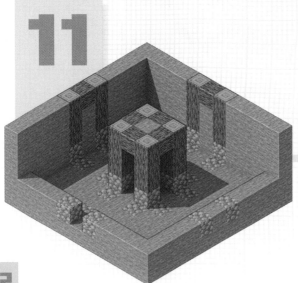

Once you're ready to complete the mine shaft, start building section 3. Excavate another 4 layers of blocks directly below your mine shaft and build the oak log and cobblestone structures into the walls.

Continue the tiered oak plank rings from step 10 until you reach the ground, just like in steps 7-8.

12

13

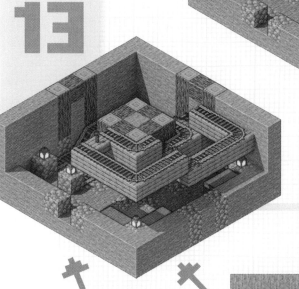

Finally, complete the railway like in steps 9-10 and place cobblestone blocks at the end of each track. Then add the finishing details with chests, lanterns and an exit.

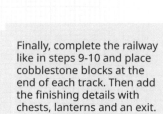

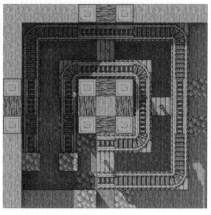

Completing steps 1-13 will run a railway 12 blocks down into the ground. When you're finished, place a mine cart on each of the rail tracks going in opposite directions. If you want to run a supply line out, place a mine cart with furnace on one of the railways.

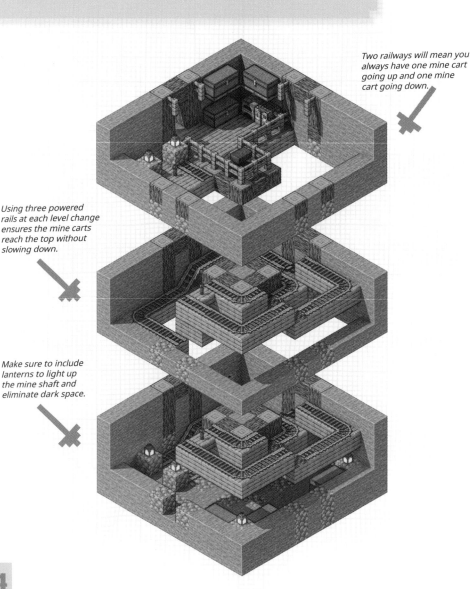

Two railways will mean you always have one mine cart going up and one mine cart going down.

Using three powered rails at each level change ensures the mine carts reach the top without slowing down.

Make sure to include lanterns to light up the mine shaft and eliminate dark space.

HOW DEEP CAN I GO?

This build is split into 3 carefully designed sections. Each section is 4 blocks tall, with section 2 designed to be repeated until you have reached your desired depth. To build the bedrock train, start by building the embarking station where your train line will begin. Next, repeat section 2, the mine shaft section, until you reach your desired depth. Finally, complete the build with section 3, the disembarking station.

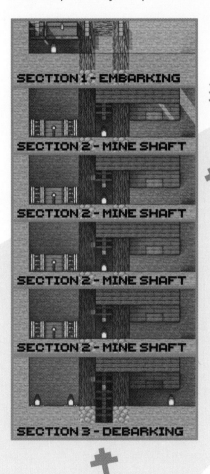

SECTION 1 - EMBARKING

SECTION 2 - MINE SHAFT

SECTION 2 - MINE SHAFT

SECTION 2 - MINE SHAFT

SECTION 2 - MINE SHAFT

SECTION 3 - DEBARKING

The first section is the embarking station, where you can enter the mine shaft.

The second section is the mine shaft that lowers you into the mine. You can repeat this section as many times as you like to go deeper and deeper underground.

This bedrock train is composed of one embarking station, 4 mine shaft sections and one disembarking station, which will take you 16 blocks deep!

The third section is the disembarking station. Climb out here to start mining!

RAINBOW STABLES

Horses are a fast and easy way to travel around Minecraft on land. All you need is a horse and saddle, and away you go! This build uses fences to keep horses from escaping their enclosures. Treat your horses to some luxury accommodation with these rainbow stables!

DIFFICULTY:
★★★★☆
🕐 30 minutes

1

Start by laying the foundation for your stables using cobblestone, grass and colored concrete. This build features stalls, a barn and a paddock.

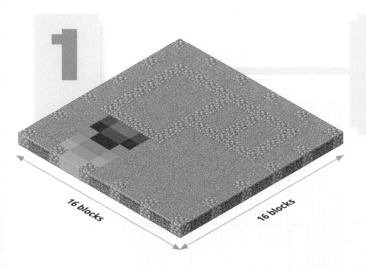

16 blocks

16 blocks

2

Next, use the cobblestone outline to start building the stable walls from purpur blocks and birch planks. Place a cauldron and fill it using a water bucket.

3

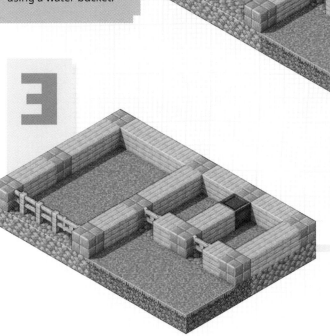

Enclose the barn and stalls with birch fences and birch fence gates.

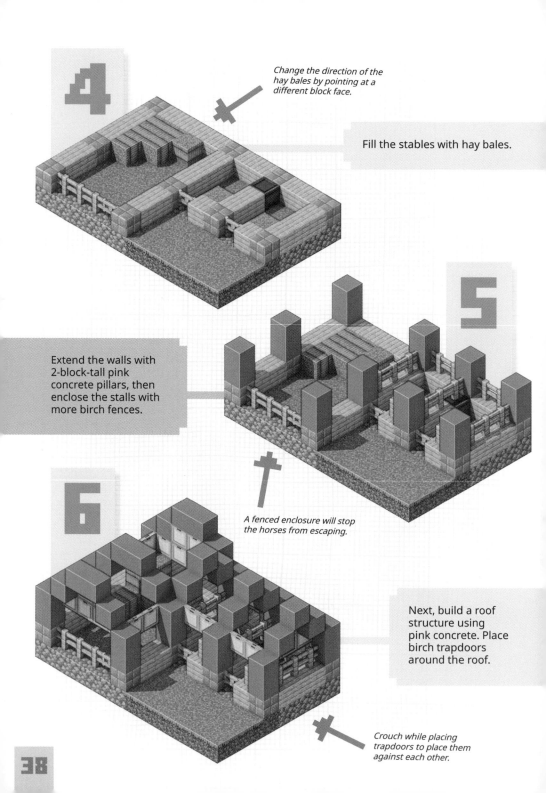

4

Change the direction of the hay bales by pointing at a different block face.

Fill the stables with hay bales.

5

Extend the walls with 2-block-tall pink concrete pillars, then enclose the stalls with more birch fences.

A fenced enclosure will stop the horses from escaping.

6

Next, build a roof structure using pink concrete. Place birch trapdoors around the roof.

Crouch while placing trapdoors to place them against each other.

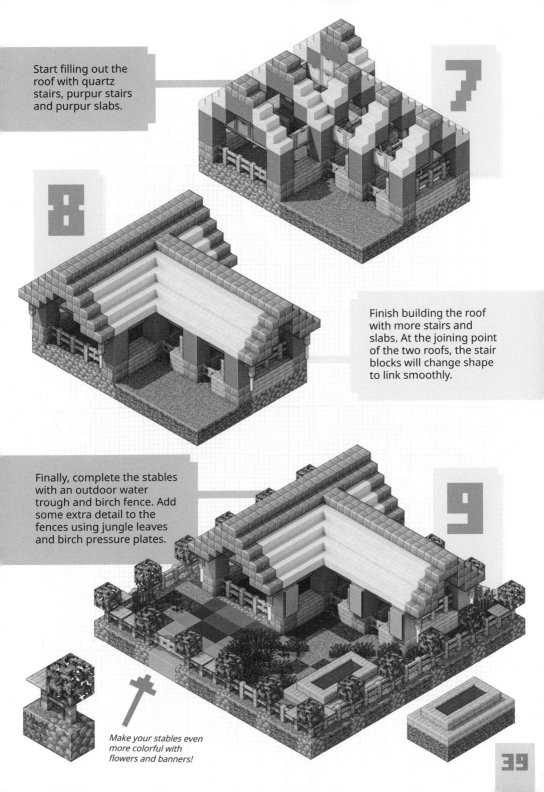

Start filling out the roof with quartz stairs, purpur stairs and purpur slabs.

7

8

Finish building the roof with more stairs and slabs. At the joining point of the two roofs, the stair blocks will change shape to link smoothly.

Finally, complete the stables with an outdoor water trough and birch fence. Add some extra detail to the fences using jungle leaves and birch pressure plates.

9

Make your stables even more colorful with flowers and banners!

MARKETPLACE STALL

Artistic banners, pumpkin pies, music discs – all this and more can be found at your local marketplace. Set up your own stall and sell your creations with this marketplace stall. Put your best wares on display and fill the chests with plentiful stock to meet the demands of your customers.

DIFFICULTY:
★★☆☆☆
🕐 10 minutes

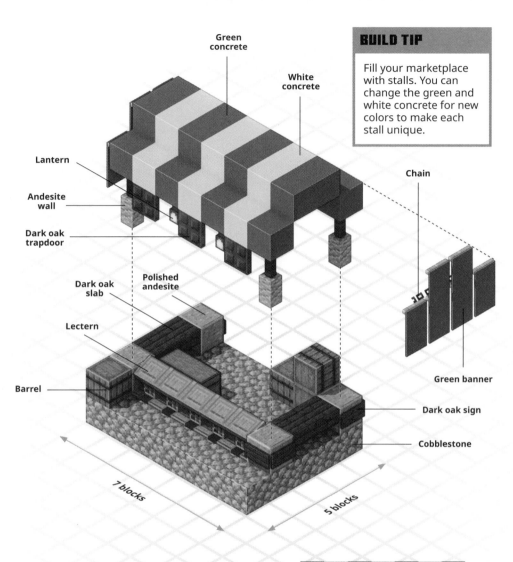

Green concrete

White concrete

Lantern

Andesite wall

Dark oak trapdoor

Dark oak slab

Polished andesite

Lectern

Barrel

Chain

Green banner

Dark oak sign

Cobblestone

7 blocks

5 blocks

BUILD TIP

Fill your marketplace with stalls. You can change the green and white concrete for new colors to make each stall unique.

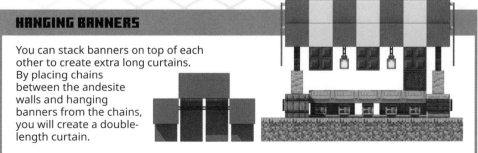

HANGING BANNERS

You can stack banners on top of each other to create extra long curtains. By placing chains between the andesite walls and hanging banners from the chains, you will create a double-length curtain.

FLOOR IS LAVA

Everyone's favorite parkour game — except the risks are real! Try your luck in this obstacle course where the floor is actually covered in lava. With small ledges, sticky honey and timed redstone circuits to navigate, you'll have to time your jumps perfectly to reach the end!

DIFFICULTY:
★★★★★
🕐 20 minutes

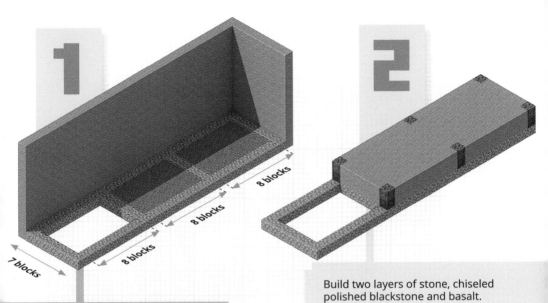

1

7 blocks

8 blocks   8 blocks   8 blocks

Start by excavating an underground chamber for your course and laying foundations using dirt and cobblestone. This course is split into three equally sized sections.

2

Build two layers of stone, chiseled polished blackstone and basalt.

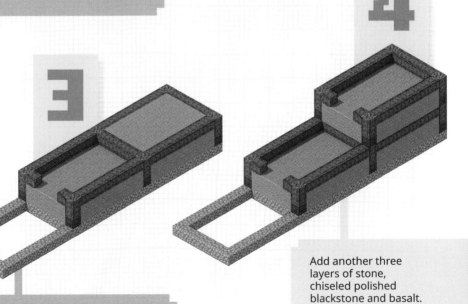

3

Add another layer of stone and basalt.

4

Add another three layers of stone, chiseled polished blackstone and basalt.

5

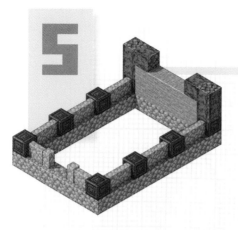

Focusing on the first section of the build, start building the walls using prismarine walls and chiseled polished blackstone.

6

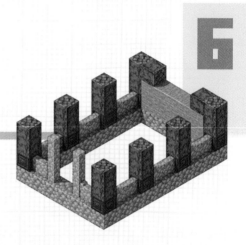

Add two basalt blocks on top of each of the chiseled polished blackstone, then create an entrance using prismarine walls.

7

Complete the first section with another layer of chiseled polished blackstone and prismarine walls.

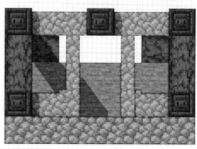

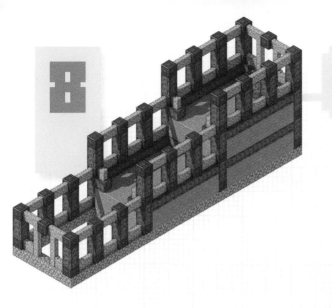

8 Next, complete the next two sections of the build using the same blocks as steps 5-7.

9

Now add lighting to the build. Place crimson trapdoors in each section of the build, then add soul lanterns below them.

10

Finally, fill the floor with lava and add obstacles for players to jump to. See the next page for obstacles you can include.

PARKOUR OBSTACLES

SET-UP CHEST

Place a chest at the start of the course and fill it with projectiles. Competitors will need to shoot the target block in the middle of the course to be able to reach the finish line.

OBSTACLE 1: STICK & SLIDE

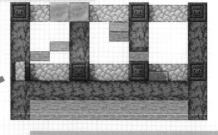

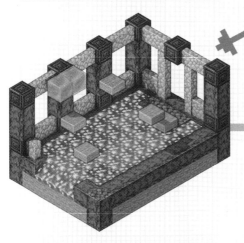

Start off simple with a jumping challenge. Place slabs and honey blocks as shown – players must climb the slabs and slide along the honey wall to reach the next section.

OBSTACLE 2: QUICK STEP

Better move fast on this obstacle! The target block is connected to two sticky pistons. These pistons will create a bridge when activated, but only for a second. Grab your bow to shoot the target block, then move quickly to reach the next section before the pistons pull the stone from beneath your feet.

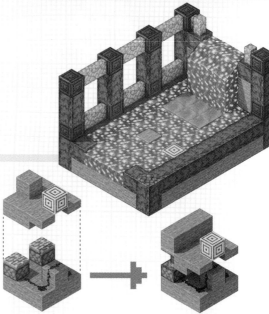

EXPLODED VIEW

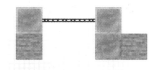

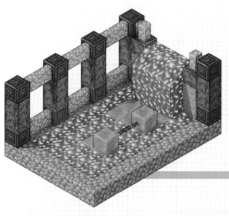

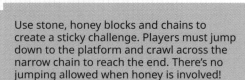

Use stone, honey blocks and chains to create a sticky challenge. Players must jump down to the platform and crawl across the narrow chain to reach the end. There's no jumping allowed when honey is involved!

FINAL BUILD

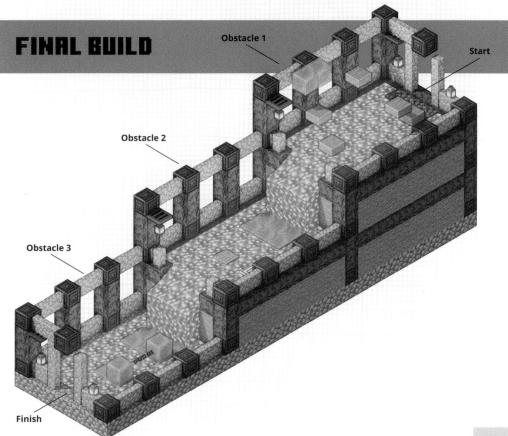

Obstacle 1

Start

Obstacle 2

Obstacle 3

Finish

47

OVE ORLD SHOW OO

Searching high and low for rare loot will take you on a journey through Minecraft's many biomes, from the deepest depths to the highest peaks. Put your collection on display with this showroom! Keep a logbook of your journeys for visiting friends, so they can read about your exploits.

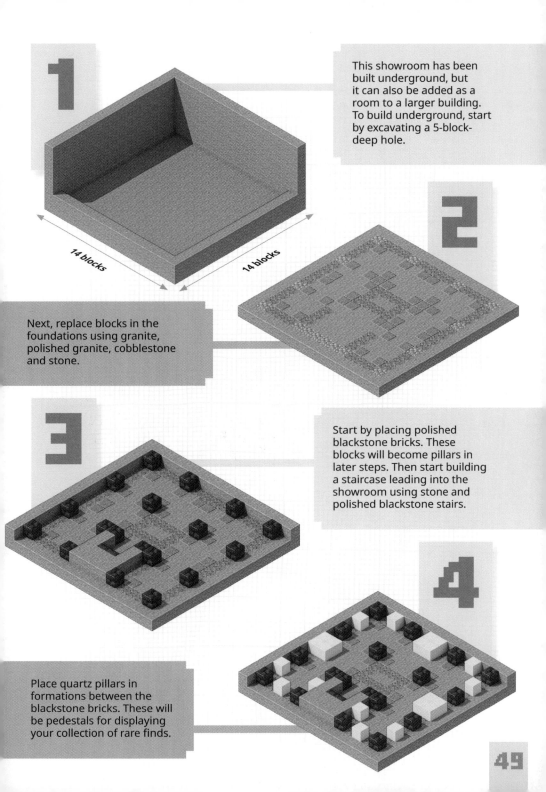

1

This showroom has been built underground, but it can also be added as a room to a larger building. To build underground, start by excavating a 5-block-deep hole.

14 blocks

14 blocks

Next, replace blocks in the foundations using granite, polished granite, cobblestone and stone.

2

3

Start by placing polished blackstone bricks. These blocks will become pillars in later steps. Then start building a staircase leading into the showroom using stone and polished blackstone stairs.

4

Place quartz pillars in formations between the blackstone bricks. These will be pedestals for displaying your collection of rare finds.

Extend the polished blackstone bricks to be 3-block-tall pillars as shown. Continue building the staircase using stone and polished blackstone stairs.

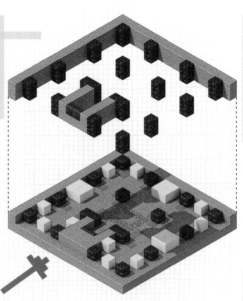

5

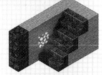

STAIRCASE

Place diorite walls against the pillars as shown, then use glowstone to light up the build. At the bottom of the staircase, place two iron doors and buttons for opening them.

6

7

Use polished blackstone stairs and polished blackstone slabs to turn each of the blackstone pillars into arches.

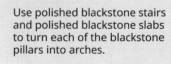

ARCH

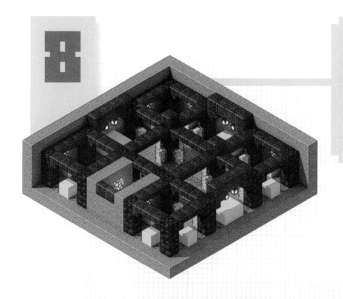

8

Finally, use polished blackstone and chiseled polished blackstone to connect the arches on each of the four walls and hang lanterns to illuminate the showroom. Then decorate your showroom – see the suggestions below!

PEDESTAL DESIGNS

You can style your showroom however you like! If you're looking for inspiration, why not try some of these fun designs. Include lecterns with books for recording your journeys and the stories of how you found each item on display.

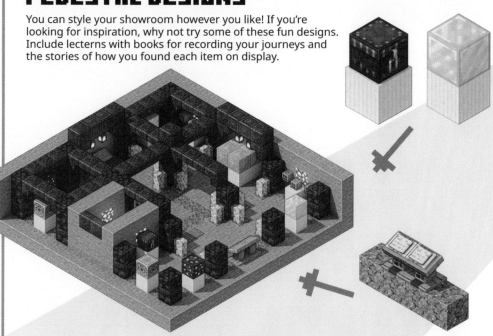

HANGING HOME

Keep an eye on the clock, for once night falls, pesky mobs will emerge to sneak up on unsuspecting players. To the night owls among us, these mobs are a nuisance – especially the creepers! Luckily, most mobs can't climb, so a hanging home is perfect for getting work done at night.

DIFFICULTY:
★★★★★
🕐 30 minutes

1

Build this hanging home beneath a natural stone bridge, or inside a large underground cavern that is at least 15 blocks underground. Once you have found a suitable location, build the home's hanging chain using grindstones, chains and jungle planks.

Change the direction of the grindstones by rotating your position around the block.

2

Start building a square-shaped frame for the roof using jungle wood.

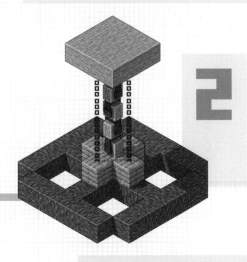

3

Place jungle slabs against the bottom half of each of the jungle planks.

4

Add two protruding 2-block-long beams from each side of the roof frame.

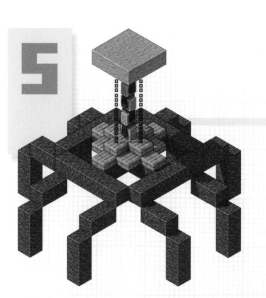

5 Add pillars to the jungle wood frame with 3-block-tall jungle wood columns as shown.

6 Build a platform below the jungle wood frame using slabs and grass blocks.

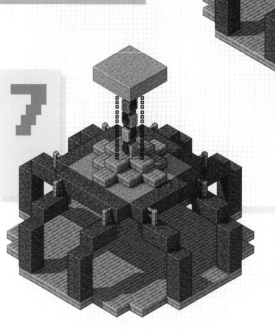

7 Next, start adding details to the hanging home. Place jungle fences on top of the frame, then fill the gaps at the top with grass blocks.

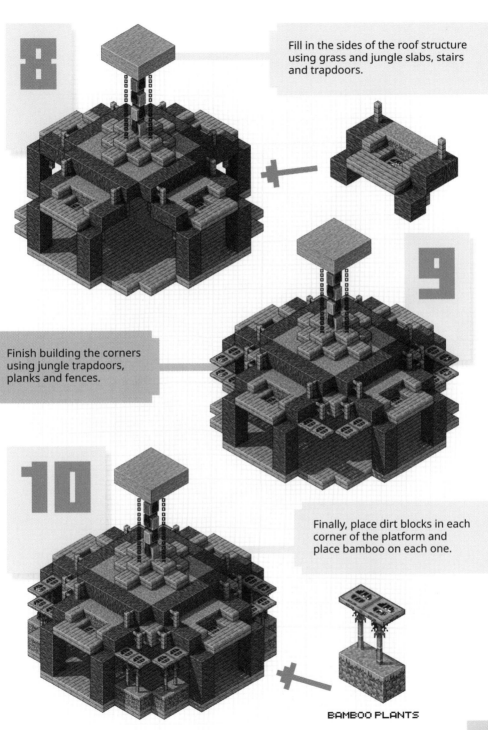

8

Fill in the sides of the roof structure using grass and jungle slabs, stairs and trapdoors.

9

Finish building the corners using jungle trapdoors, planks and fences.

10

Finally, place dirt blocks in each corner of the platform and place bamboo on each one.

BAMBOO PLANTS

HOUSEHOLD ESSENTIALS

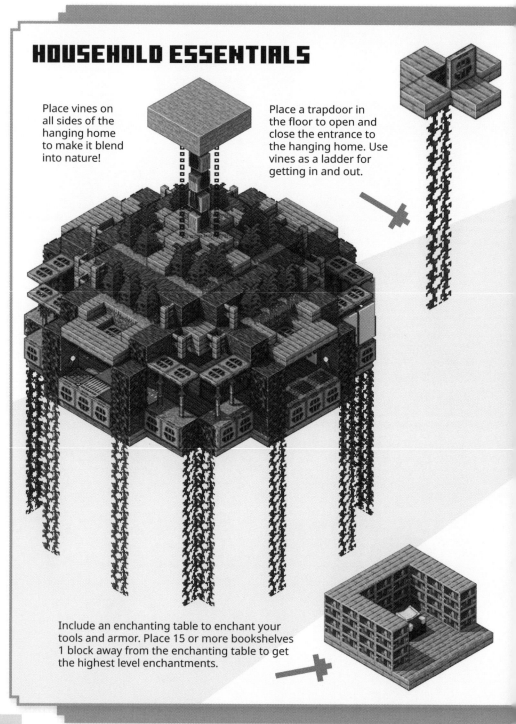

Place vines on all sides of the hanging home to make it blend into nature!

Place a trapdoor in the floor to open and close the entrance to the hanging home. Use vines as a ladder for getting in and out.

Include an enchanting table to enchant your tools and armor. Place 15 or more bookshelves 1 block away from the enchanting table to get the highest level enchantments.

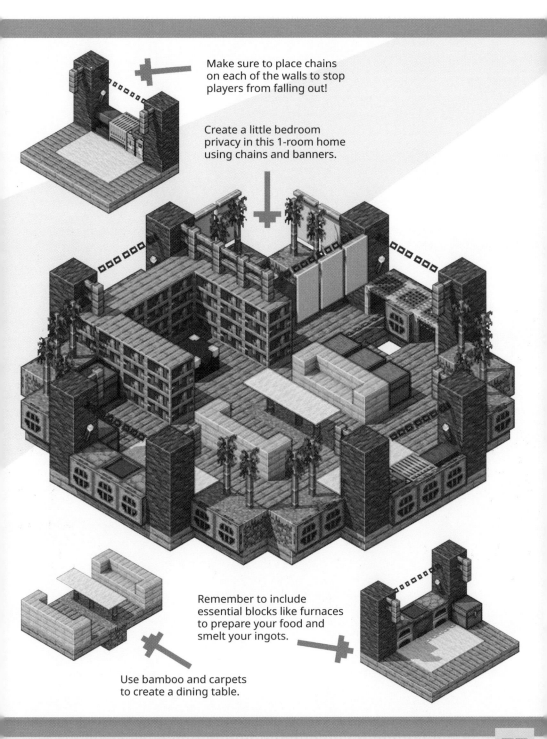

Make sure to place chains on each of the walls to stop players from falling out!

Create a little bedroom privacy in this 1-room home using chains and banners.

Remember to include essential blocks like furnaces to prepare your food and smelt your ingots.

Use bamboo and carpets to create a dining table.

TRADER SLEIGH

Icy biomes are scarce in resources, making them an ideal place to sell your surplus blocks for stacks of shiny green emeralds. This sleigh is packed with storage to fit all your trading needs – just set up shop, lower the trapdoors and call out to nearby players in need of rare resources.

DIFFICULTY:
★★★☆☆
🕐 15 minutes

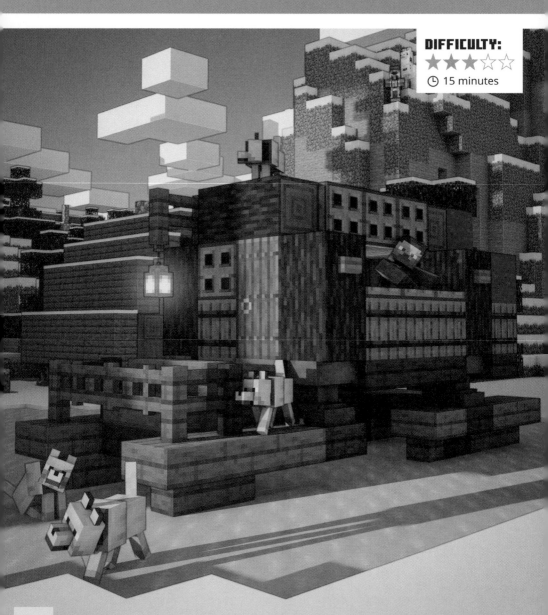

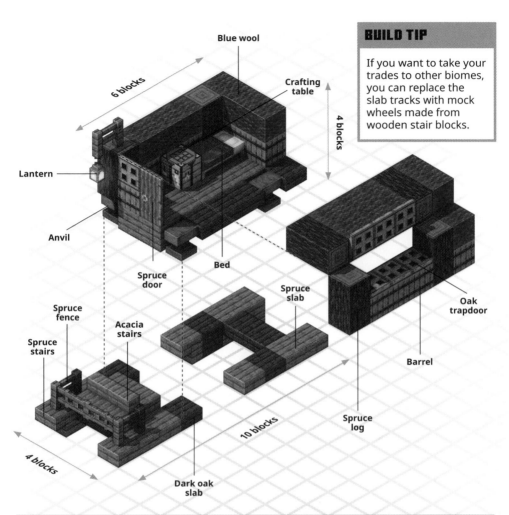

Blue wool

Crafting table

6 blocks

4 blocks

BUILD TIP

If you want to take your trades to other biomes, you can replace the slab tracks with mock wheels made from wooden stair blocks.

Lantern

Anvil

Spruce door

Bed

Spruce slab

Oak trapdoor

Barrel

Spruce fence

Acacia stairs

Spruce stairs

10 blocks

Spruce log

4 blocks

Dark oak slab

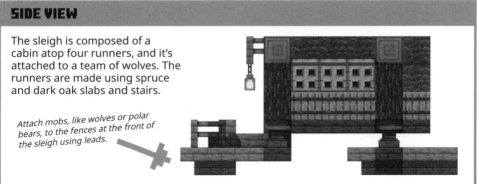

SIDE VIEW

The sleigh is composed of a cabin atop four runners, and it's attached to a team of wolves. The runners are made using spruce and dark oak slabs and stairs.

Attach mobs, like wolves or polar bears, to the fences at the front of the sleigh using leads.

SPACE ROCKET

First you explored the Overworld. Then you ventured into the Nether.
Soon you found yourself traveling the End. Next stop: outer space!
Get ready to travel to worlds unknown in your very own space rocket!
This domed build is your ticket to the stars.

DIFFICULTY:
★★☆☆☆
🕐 15 minutes

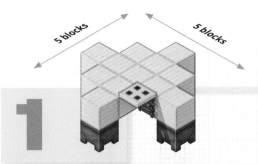

5 blocks   5 blocks

Start by creating the feet for your rocket using cauldrons and blocks of iron. Place an iron trapdoor and ladder for climbing in and out.

1

Begin building the sides of your rocket. First place a ring of gray concrete blocks. Then add a button beside the ladder and another button inside the rocket beside the trapdoor.

2

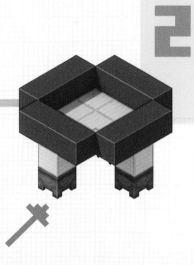

3

Add another two layers of blocks, as you did in step 2, using orange concrete and blocks of iron.

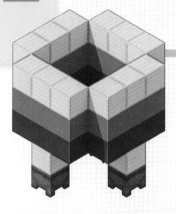

4

Create a floor using smooth stone slabs. Then join the two levels together with ladders.

5

Continue building the rocket walls with three more layers of orange concrete. Place four black stained glass windows.

6

Build another floor using smooth stone slabs, as in step 4. Then join the floors together with more ladders.

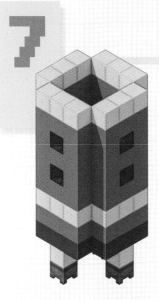

7

Add another three layers to the rocket using orange concrete, blocks of iron and black stained glass.

8

SIDE VIEW

Next, start creating the rocket's nose cone. Place blocks of iron and gray concrete on each side as shown.

9

LEG

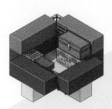

Finish building the nose cone using the same blocks. Then create four legs for the rocket using more gray concrete and blocks of iron.

10

Finally, add the finishing touches to your rocket. Place trapdoors on top of each of the gray concrete blocks and add iron bars and buttons between the rocket legs.

SPACE ESSENTIALS

With limited room aboard your rocket, it's vital you pack only the necessities. Be sure to have a cartography table for charting the stars as you travel to new faraway worlds.

JUNGLE SHRINE

Intrepid explorers are always finding long-lost structures in overgrown jungles. These mysterious buildings can offer an insight into forgotten times and show how ancient civilizations used to live. Build a shrine for future explorers to find – how will you impress them?

DIFFICULTY:
★★★★☆
🕐 30 minutes

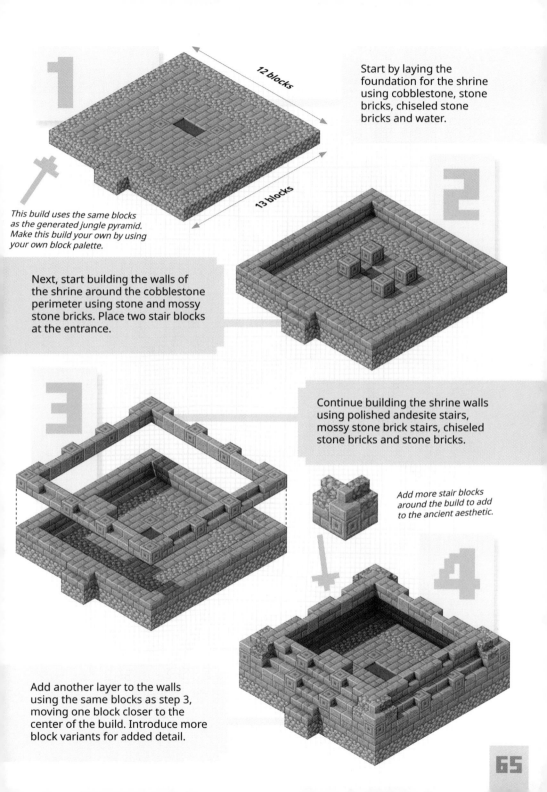

1

12 blocks

13 blocks

Start by laying the foundation for the shrine using cobblestone, stone bricks, chiseled stone bricks and water.

This build uses the same blocks as the generated jungle pyramid. Make this build your own by using your own block palette.

2

Next, start building the walls of the shrine around the cobblestone perimeter using stone and mossy stone bricks. Place two stair blocks at the entrance.

3

Continue building the shrine walls using polished andesite stairs, mossy stone brick stairs, chiseled stone bricks and stone bricks.

Add more stair blocks around the build to add to the ancient aesthetic.

4

Add another layer to the walls using the same blocks as step 3, moving one block closer to the center of the build. Introduce more block variants for added detail.

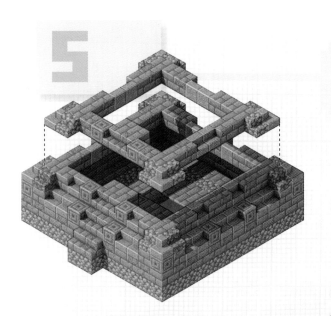

5

Add another layer of blocks as before, moving another block closer to the center.

6

Add another layer of blocks, bringing the layer closer to the center again.

7

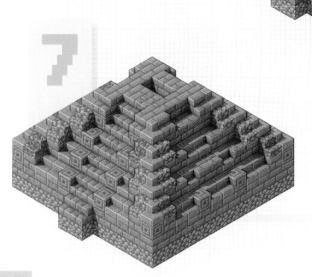

Build a final layer of blocks, leaving a small gap in the center. This gap will become a vine ladder entrance in step 9.

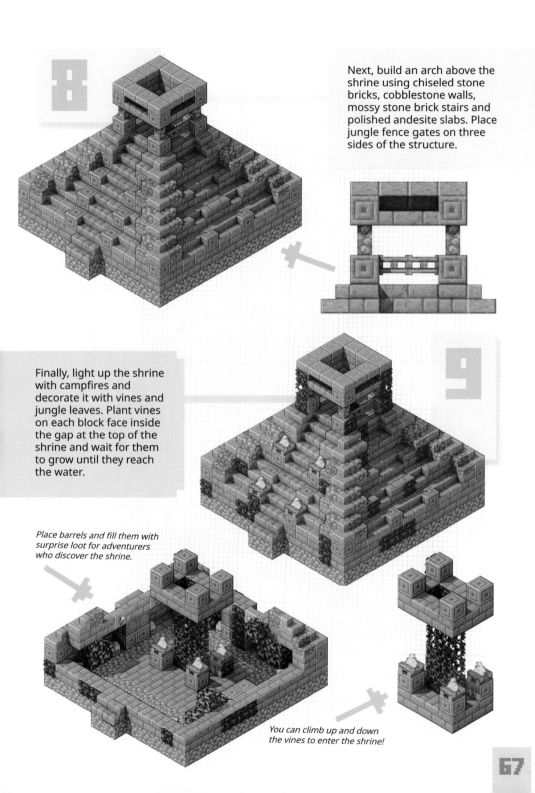

Next, build an arch above the shrine using chiseled stone bricks, cobblestone walls, mossy stone brick stairs and polished andesite slabs. Place jungle fence gates on three sides of the structure.

Finally, light up the shrine with campfires and decorate it with vines and jungle leaves. Plant vines on each block face inside the gap at the top of the shrine and wait for them to grow until they reach the water.

Place barrels and fill them with surprise loot for adventurers who discover the shrine.

You can climb up and down the vines to enter the shrine!

SUPER SLIDE

Ready. Set. Go! Grab a boat from the chest and place it on the ice. Jump in, start paddling and see who moves the fastest – the last player to the finish line loses and has to return the boats to the chest. This build takes advantage of the different block effects to create fun carnival rides.

DIFFICULTY:
★★☆☆☆
🕐 15 minutes

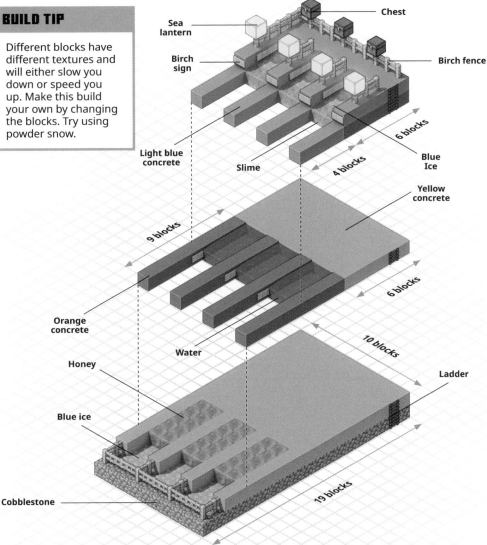

BUILD TIP

Different blocks have different textures and will either slow you down or speed you up. Make this build your own by changing the blocks. Try using powder snow.

Chest

Sea lantern

Birch sign

Birch fence

Light blue concrete

Slime

Blue Ice

6 blocks

4 blocks

Yellow concrete

9 blocks

6 blocks

Orange concrete

Water

10 blocks

Honey

Ladder

Blue ice

Cobblestone

19 blocks

LONGER AND TALLER

Want to create a super-duper slide? Make your slide longer and longer! The more blocks you add, the longer your ride will last. You can even add more layers to make a taller slide for the most daring friends.

CONCERT STAGE

Throw the biggest block party your friends have ever seen! Bust out some sweet dance moves as you listen to the latest hits. Whether you're jamming on your new guitar or setting the beat with a killer set of drums, crank that volume to the top and put on the show of a lifetime!

DIFFICULTY:
★★★☆☆
🕐 25 minutes

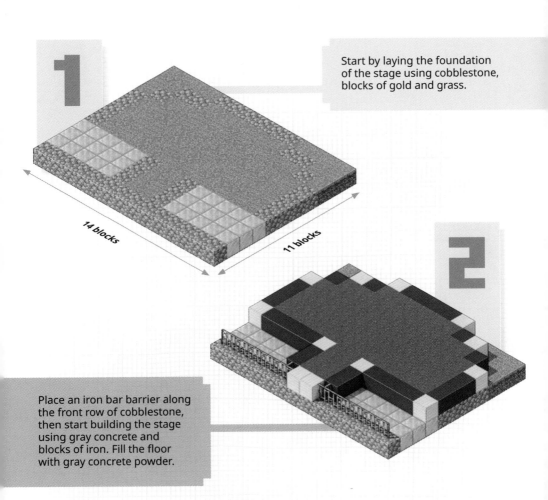

1

Start by laying the foundation of the stage using cobblestone, blocks of gold and grass.

14 blocks

11 blocks

2

Place an iron bar barrier along the front row of cobblestone, then start building the stage using gray concrete and blocks of iron. Fill the floor with gray concrete powder.

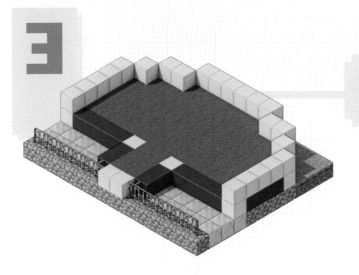

3

Extend the back and side walls of the stage using blocks of iron.

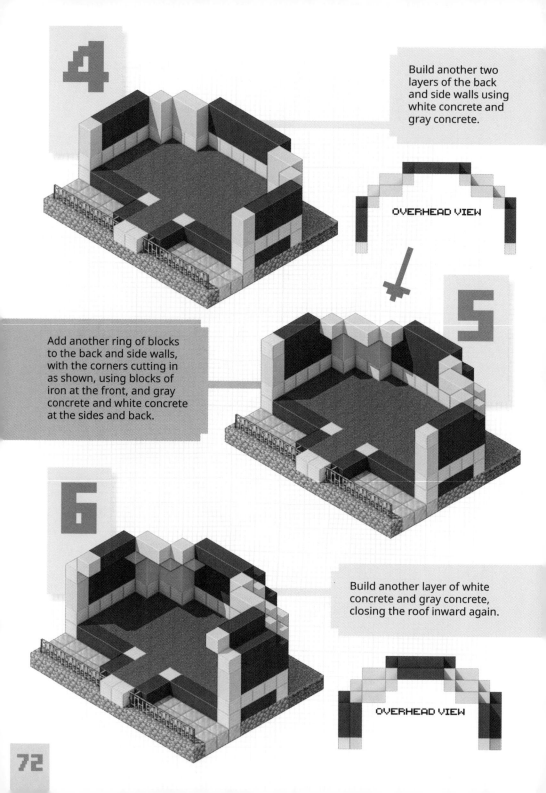

4

Build another two layers of the back and side walls using white concrete and gray concrete.

OVERHEAD VIEW

5

Add another ring of blocks to the back and side walls, with the corners cutting in as shown, using blocks of iron at the front, and gray concrete and white concrete at the sides and back.

6

Build another layer of white concrete and gray concrete, closing the roof inward again.

OVERHEAD VIEW

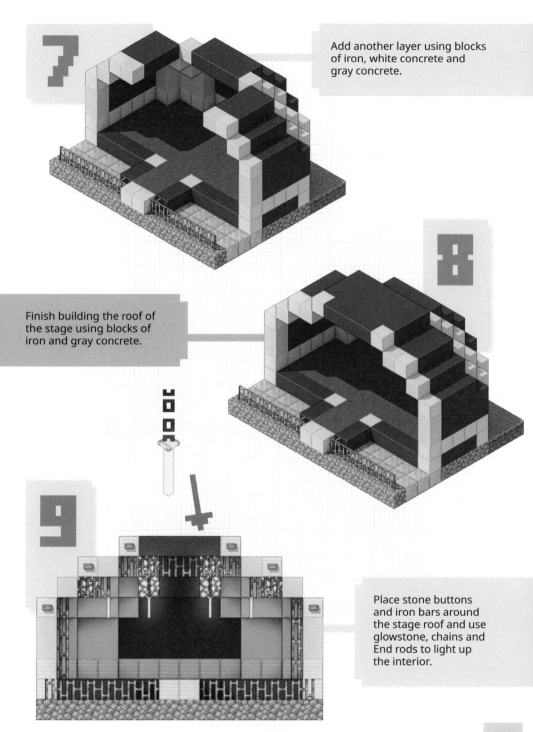

7 Add another layer using blocks of iron, white concrete and gray concrete.

Finish building the roof of the stage using blocks of iron and gray concrete.

8

9 Place stone buttons and iron bars around the stage roof and use glowstone, chains and End rods to light up the interior.

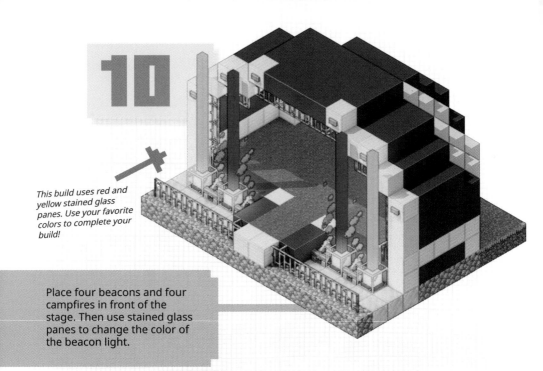

10

This build uses red and yellow stained glass panes. Use your favorite colors to complete your build!

Place four beacons and four campfires in front of the stage. Then use stained glass panes to change the color of the beacon light.

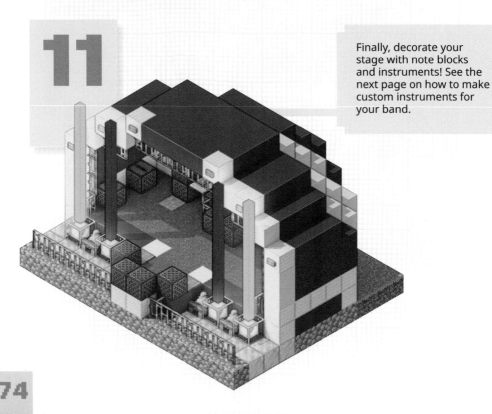

11

Finally, decorate your stage with note blocks and instruments! See the next page on how to make custom instruments for your band.

INSTRUMENTS

Now that your stage is built, it's time to create some sounds for the band. Check out some of the instruments below.

STRING BASS

BASS DRUM

CHIMES

FLUTE

GUITAR

XYLOPHONE

BANJO

DIDGERIDOO

HARP/ PIANO

Pick your instruments and spread them around the stage. Choose a note from the grid above and place the corresponding block below the note block. When you step on the pressure plate, the note will play!

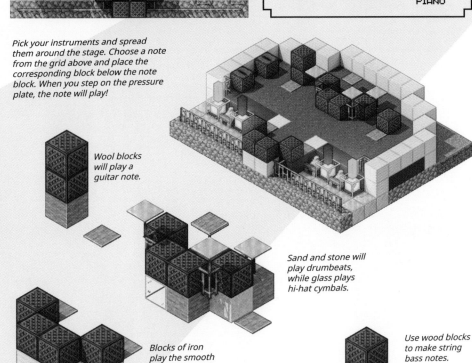

Wool blocks will play a guitar note.

Sand and stone will play drumbeats, while glass plays hi-hat cymbals.

Blocks of iron play the smooth xylophone, and the blocks of gold a ringing bell.

Use wood blocks to make string bass notes.

LIGHTHOUSE

Craggy coastlines and shallow waters are the bane of ships caught in storms. Historically, civilizations have built light signals to warn ships of impending dangers. You can do the same! Build this lighthouse with a revolving redstone light to keep players safe from hazardous waters.

DIFFICULTY:
★★★☆☆
🕐 20 minutes

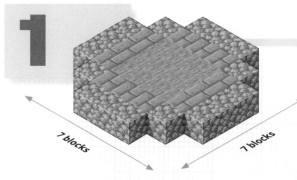

1

Start by laying the foundation for your lighthouse using cobblestone, stone and stone bricks.

7 blocks

7 blocks

2

Next, start building the lighthouse walls using stone bricks, leaving a gap in one wall.

Did you know you can use concrete powder to build? Just pour water over it when you're done and the powder will turn to concrete.

3

Continue building the lighthouse using stone bricks, chiseled stone bricks and red concrete, leaving a space for a doorway.

4

Add another four layers of red concrete to the walls as shown. Then place a dark oak door in the doorway.

5

Moving a block inward, narrowing the walls, place a ring of white concrete as shown.

Place another 5 layers of white concrete walls, leaving gaps for windows. Place glass panes in the gaps.

6

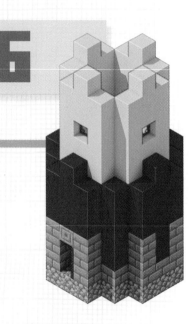

7

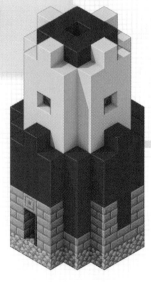

Move another block inward and place a 3x3 ring of red concrete.

If you're building with concrete powder, first place temporary blocks below the ring. This will stop the concrete powder from falling with gravity.

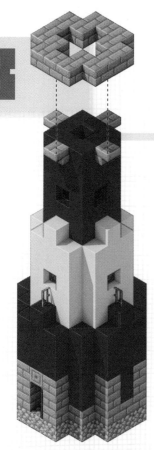

8

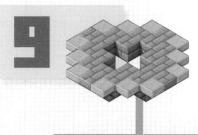

Add another 5 layers of red concrete, then place stone bricks and stone brick stairs at the top of the lighthouse as shown. Add iron bars and glass panes.

9

Place a ring of stone brick slabs and smooth stone slabs around on top of the structure.

Observers have arrows on their top face – use these to make sure they're facing the right way

10

Next, place a ring of observers as shown, using the arrows as a guide.

11

Add stone bricks and white concrete around the observers.

12

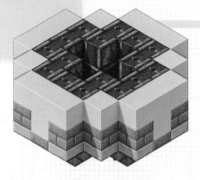

Add a layer of downward-facing observers directly above the observers in step 10, then place a ring of white concrete around them.

13

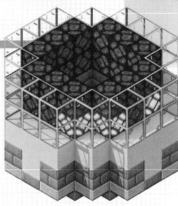

Add two layers of redstone lamps on top of the observers, then surround them with glass blocks.

14

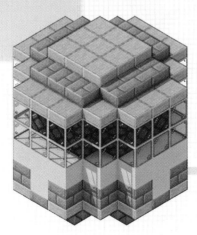

Finally, complete the lighthouse structure with a roof made of smooth stone slabs and stone bricks.

INTERIORS

There's limited space inside the lighthouse, so better make good use of it! Build a ladder to reach the redstone observers, and place some essential survival blocks at the base.

Keep a campfire burning to stay warm – those ocean winds will put a chill into your bones.

Create a spiral staircase and connect it to a ladder. You'll need to be able to access the observers in case something goes wrong!

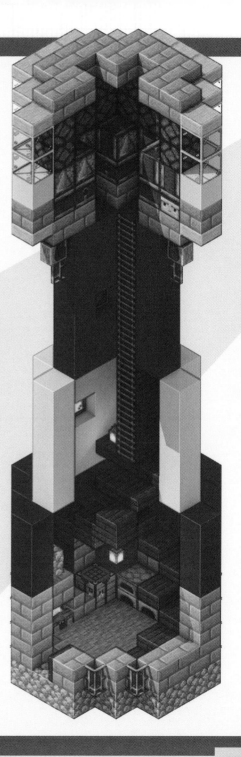

CLUCK-CLUCK COOP

Need some eggs? Create your own chicken coop for our favorite Minecraft bird. This build will give your pet chickens the life of luxury they deserve, while hoppers automatically collect all the eggs you could want. What will you do with so many eggs?

DIFFICULTY:
★★★☆☆
🕐 20 minutes

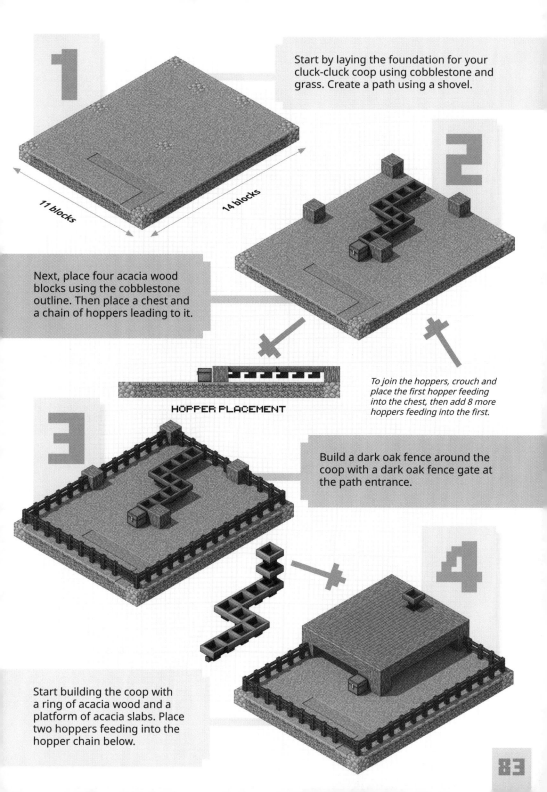

1

Start by laying the foundation for your cluck-cluck coop using cobblestone and grass. Create a path using a shovel.

11 blocks

14 blocks

2

Next, place four acacia wood blocks using the cobblestone outline. Then place a chest and a chain of hoppers leading to it.

HOPPER PLACEMENT

To join the hoppers, crouch and place the first hopper feeding into the chest, then add 8 more hoppers feeding into the first.

3

Build a dark oak fence around the coop with a dark oak fence gate at the path entrance.

4

Start building the coop with a ring of acacia wood and a platform of acacia slabs. Place two hoppers feeding into the hopper chain below.

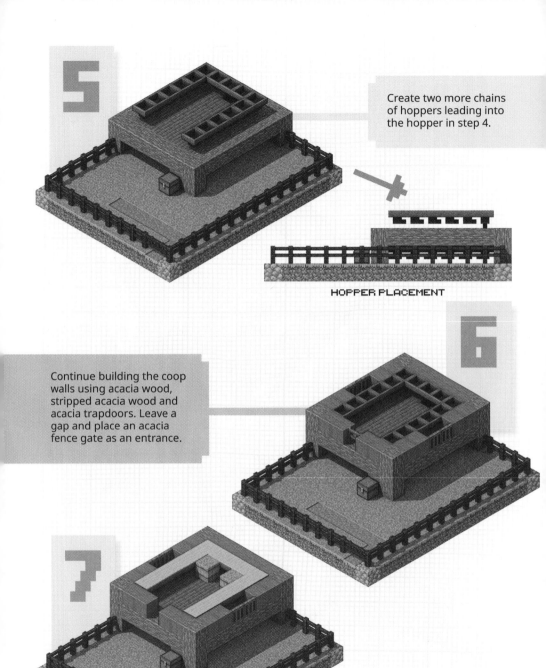

5

Create two more chains of hoppers leading into the hopper in step 4.

HOPPER PLACEMENT

Continue building the coop walls using acacia wood, stripped acacia wood and acacia trapdoors. Leave a gap and place an acacia fence gate as an entrance.

6

7

Place yellow carpets on each of the hoppers. Then add two hay bales inside the coop.

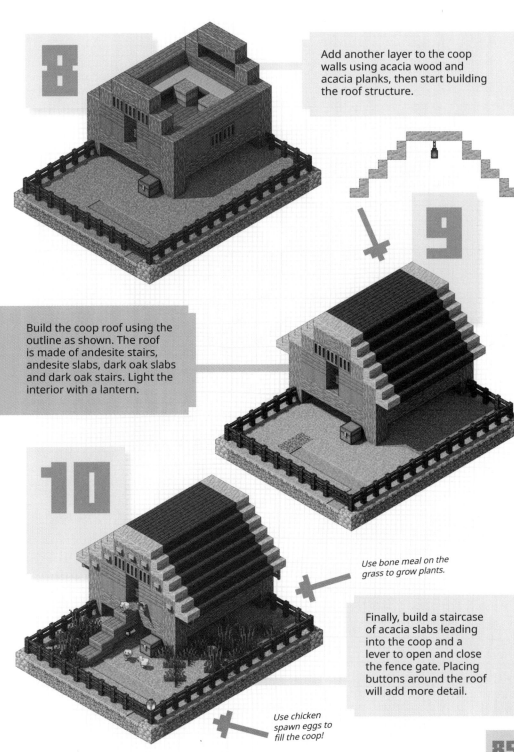

8

Add another layer to the coop walls using acacia wood and acacia planks, then start building the roof structure.

9

Build the coop roof using the outline as shown. The roof is made of andesite stairs, andesite slabs, dark oak slabs and dark oak stairs. Light the interior with a lantern.

10

Use bone meal on the grass to grow plants.

Finally, build a staircase of acacia slabs leading into the coop and a lever to open and close the fence gate. Placing buttons around the roof will add more detail.

Use chicken spawn eggs to fill the coop!

NORSE LONGHOUSE

Embrace your inner Norse spirit while conquering new lands with this longhouse. Did you know that in the Middle Ages Vikings would live in large communal longhouses like this? These halls provided housing and feasts for groups of Vikings when they returned from their voyages.

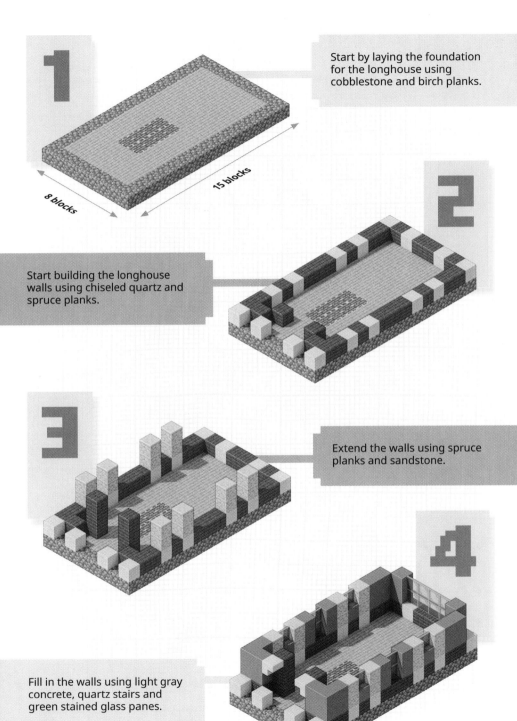

1 Start by laying the foundation for the longhouse using cobblestone and birch planks.

8 blocks

15 blocks

2 Start building the longhouse walls using chiseled quartz and spruce planks.

3 Extend the walls using spruce planks and sandstone.

4 Fill in the walls using light gray concrete, quartz stairs and green stained glass panes.

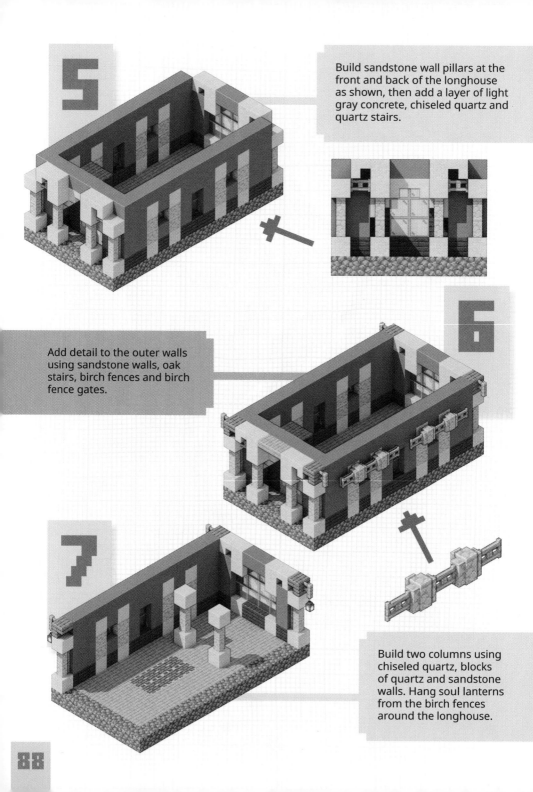

5

Build sandstone wall pillars at the front and back of the longhouse as shown, then add a layer of light gray concrete, chiseled quartz and quartz stairs.

Add detail to the outer walls using sandstone walls, oak stairs, birch fences and birch fence gates.

6

7

Build two columns using chiseled quartz, blocks of quartz and sandstone walls. Hang soul lanterns from the birch fences around the longhouse.

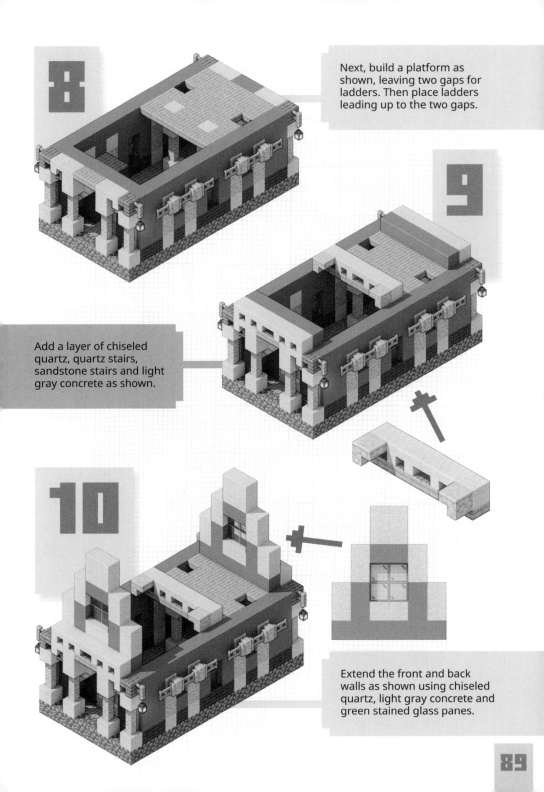

8

Next, build a platform as shown, leaving two gaps for ladders. Then place ladders leading up to the two gaps.

9

Add a layer of chiseled quartz, quartz stairs, sandstone stairs and light gray concrete as shown.

10

Extend the front and back walls as shown using chiseled quartz, light gray concrete and green stained glass panes.

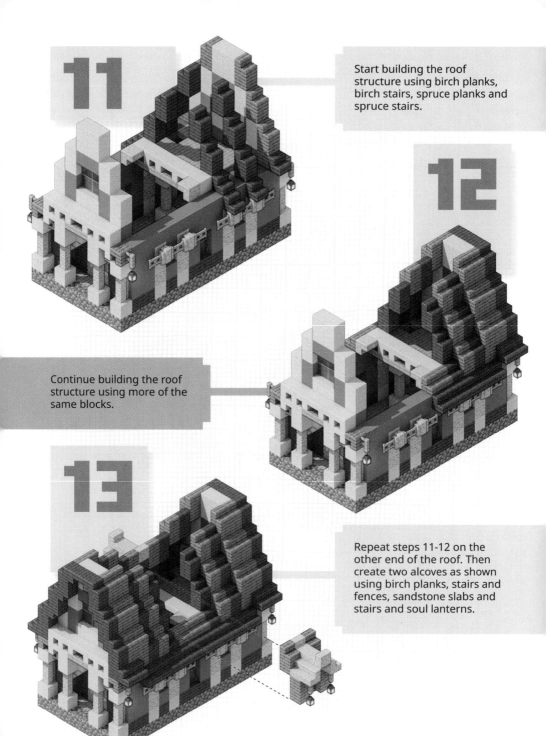

11

Start building the roof structure using birch planks, birch stairs, spruce planks and spruce stairs.

12

Continue building the roof structure using more of the same blocks.

13

Repeat steps 11-12 on the other end of the roof. Then create two alcoves as shown using birch planks, stairs and fences, sandstone slabs and stairs and soul lanterns.

14

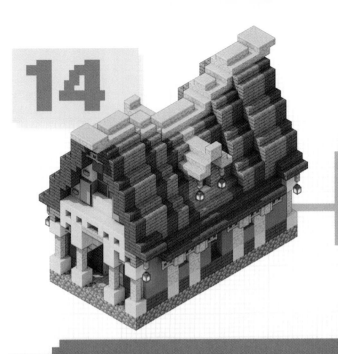

Finally, seal the top of the roof using sandstone stairs. Add some finishing touches with banners, buttons and birch fences.

INTERIOR DECORATION

Make your longhouse fit for a feast! From dining tables to bunk beds, you'll find everything you need for a merry celebration.

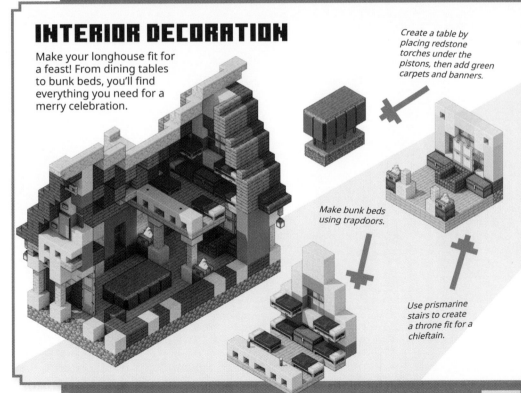

Create a table by placing redstone torches under the pistons, then add green carpets and banners.

Make bunk beds using trapdoors.

Use prismarine stairs to create a throne fit for a chieftain.

COMBINATION CHALLENGES

Congratulations, you've completed all the builds in this book. You must be quite the builder. But you're not done yet! Let's see if you're up for new challenge: combining builds together to create new ones.

Listed below are a series of combination challenges. For each of these challenges, we want you to combine the builds using the guides and build tips included in this book. How you combine the builds is completely up to you: you can resize the builds, pick new blocks or improve the design as you see fit.

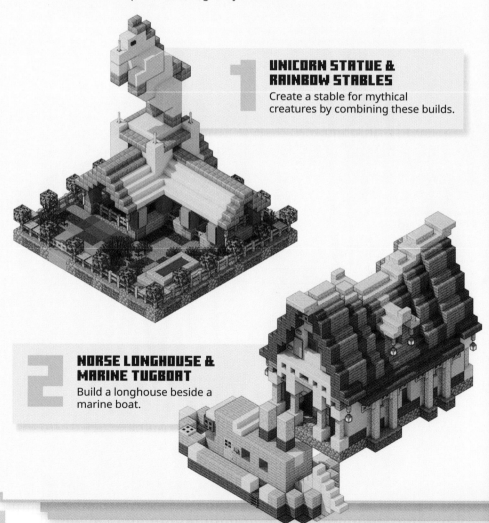

1 UNICORN STATUE & RAINBOW STABLES

Create a stable for mythical creatures by combining these builds.

2 NORSE LONGHOUSE & MARINE TUGBOAT

Build a longhouse beside a marine boat.

3 BEE HAVEN & CLUCK-CLUCK COOP

Prepare an animal habitat with a cluck-cluck coop and bee haven.

4 FLOOR IS LAVA & SUPER SLIDE

Put these builds together to make a super-fun racetrack for your friends.

5 SIDEWALK CAFE & MARKETPLACE STALL

Create a food garden with the sidewalk cafe and marketplace stalls.

GOODBYE

And that's it for today, folks! Together, we've created new homes for our favorite mobs, built new beautiful bases to live in and opened up a very hip restaurant to feed the ever-hungry villagers. They sure like their carrots.

Now it's up to you to get creative and make these builds your own. Each of these builds is ripe for innovation – use the guides and see how you can adapt them to better fit your world and needs. Maybe you have more items to showcase, or new mob-infested mountain caverns in need of a larger hanging home.

Remember, there's no right or wrong way to create in Minecraft. All ideas are good ideas! This is your game, and you are the master of your world. So until next time, keep crafting, creating and developing. Have fun and follow your imagination wherever it takes you!

DISCOVER MORE MINECRAFT:
LEVEL UP YOUR GAME WITH THE OFFICIAL GUIDES

MORE MINECRAFT:

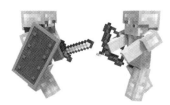

Penguin
Random
House

© 2022 Mojang AB. TM Microsoft Corporation.